Alfred's Basic Piano 1

Piano

Ear Training Book
Level 4

Gayle Kowalchyk • E. L. Lancaster

Instructions for Use

1. This EAR TRAINING BOOK is designed to be used with Alfred's Basic Piano Library, LESSON BOOK 4.

2. This book is coordinated page-by-page with the LESSON BOOK, and assignments are ideally made according to the instructions in the upper right corner of each page of the EAR TRAINING BOOK.

3. Many students enjoy completing these pages so much that they will want to go beyond the assigned material. However, it is best to wait until the indicated pages in the LESSON BOOK have been covered before the corresponding material in this book is studied.

4. This EAR TRAINING BOOK reinforces each concept presented in the LESSON BOOK and specifically focuses on the training and development of the ear. Rhythmic, melodic and intervallic concepts are drilled throughout the book to provide the necessary systematic reinforcement for the student.

5. Each page is designed to be completed using approximately five minutes of the lesson time. Examples for each page are given for the teacher (pages 38–48).

$\frac{6}{8}$ Time Signature

1. Your teacher will clap a rhythm pattern.
   Circle the pattern that you hear.

2. Your teacher will play melodies and chords in D minor. Review Lesson Book 3, page 40.
   Write the Roman numeral names ($\mathbf{i}$, $\mathbf{iv}$ or $\mathbf{V^7}$) on the lines below the staff.

1a

1b

1c

1d

2a

2b

2c

4

Use with pages 4–5.

Eighth Note Triplets

1. Your teacher will clap a rhythm pattern.
   Draw the missing notes in the third measure, using  or
2. Your teacher will play **i**, **iv** and **V⁷** chords in the key of A minor. Review Lesson Book 3, page 36.
   Write the Roman numeral name for each chord. The first chord is shown.

1a

1b

1c

1d

2a   <u> **i** </u>   _____   _____   _____

2b   <u> **iv** </u>   _____   _____   _____

2c   <u> **V7** </u>   _____   _____   _____

2d   <u> **i** </u>   _____   _____   _____

TEACHER: See page 38.

TRIADS: The 1st Inversion

1. Your teacher will play a chord progression.
   Circle the progression that you hear.

2. Your teacher will play a BLOCK chord followed by a BROKEN chord.
   Write the notes of the BROKEN chord in the order that they are played, using QUARTER NOTES.

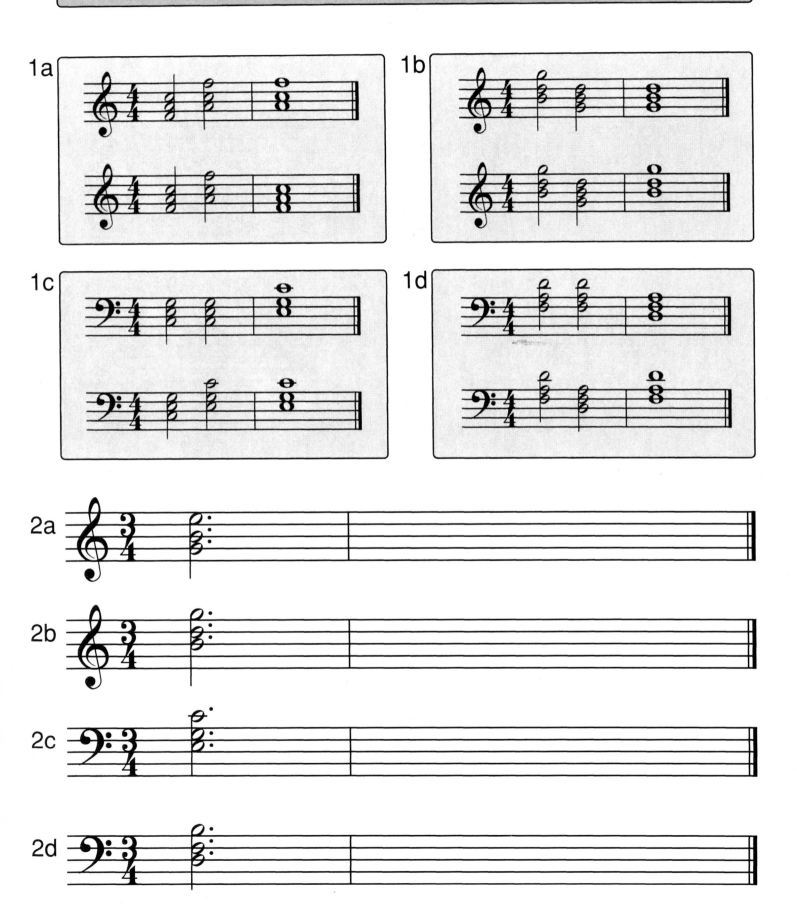

Use with pages 8–9.

Arpeggiated Chords

1. Your teacher will play four chords. Draw a wavy line beside the chord if it is ARPEGGIATED (broken or rolled).

2. Your teacher will play four melodies. Each melody contains a *ritardando*. Add the *rit.* below the staff when the tempo begins to GRADUALLY SLOW DOWN.

TRIADS: The 2nd Inversion

1. Your teacher will play a chord progression.
   Circle the progression that you hear.

2. Your teacher will play a BLOCK chord followed by a BROKEN chord.
   Write the notes of the BROKEN chord in the order that they are played, using QUARTER NOTES.

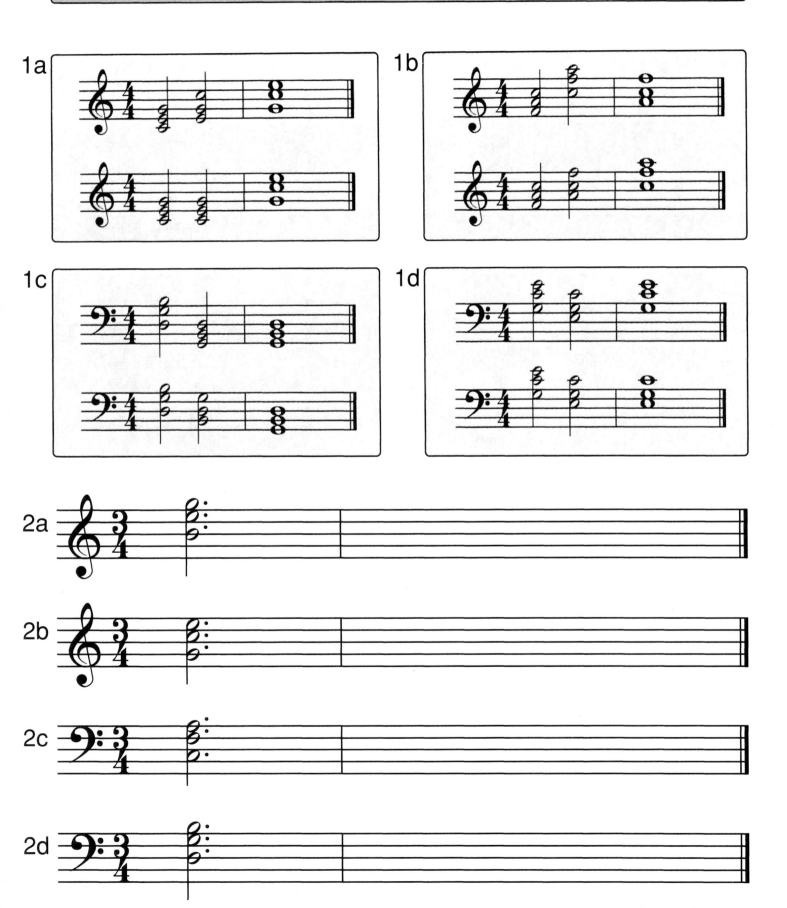

TRIADS: The 2nd Inversion

1. Your teacher will play a BROKEN chord.
   Circle the chord that you hear.

2. Your teacher will play a MELODIC interval of a 4th or 6th ABOVE the given note.
   • Draw the second note on the staff, using a half note.
   • Write the interval name (4 or 6) on the line.

1a

1b

1c

1d

2a

2b

2c
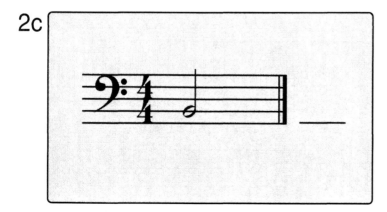

2d
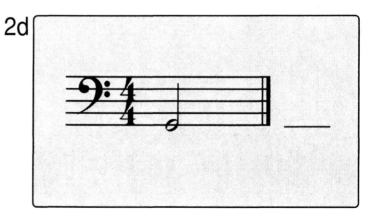

Eighth Note Triplets

1. Your teacher will play melodies that use EIGHTH NOTE TRIPLETS.
   Draw the missing notes in the third measure, using the correct rhythm.

2. Your teacher will play four chord patterns.
   Each pattern contains two ACCENTS. Add an ACCENT SIGN under or over
   the notes that are played LOUDER.

Use with page 14.

Triads in All Positions

1. Your teacher will play a chord progression.
   Circle the progression that you hear.

2. Your teacher will play a BLOCK chord followed by a BROKEN chord.
   Write the notes of the BROKEN chord in the order that they are played, using QUARTER NOTES.

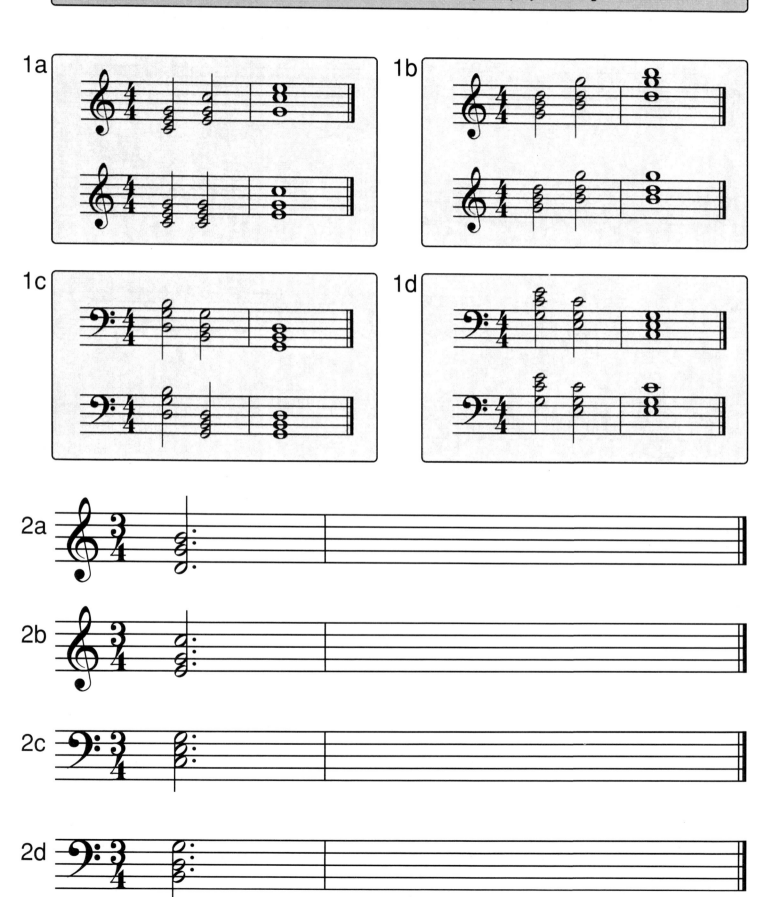

TRIADS: The 1st Inversion

1. Your teacher will play ROOT POSITION or 1st INVERSION chords.
   Circle the example that you hear.

2. Your teacher will play intervals of a 3rd or 6th.
   Circle the interval that you hear. Write the interval name (3 or 6) on the line.

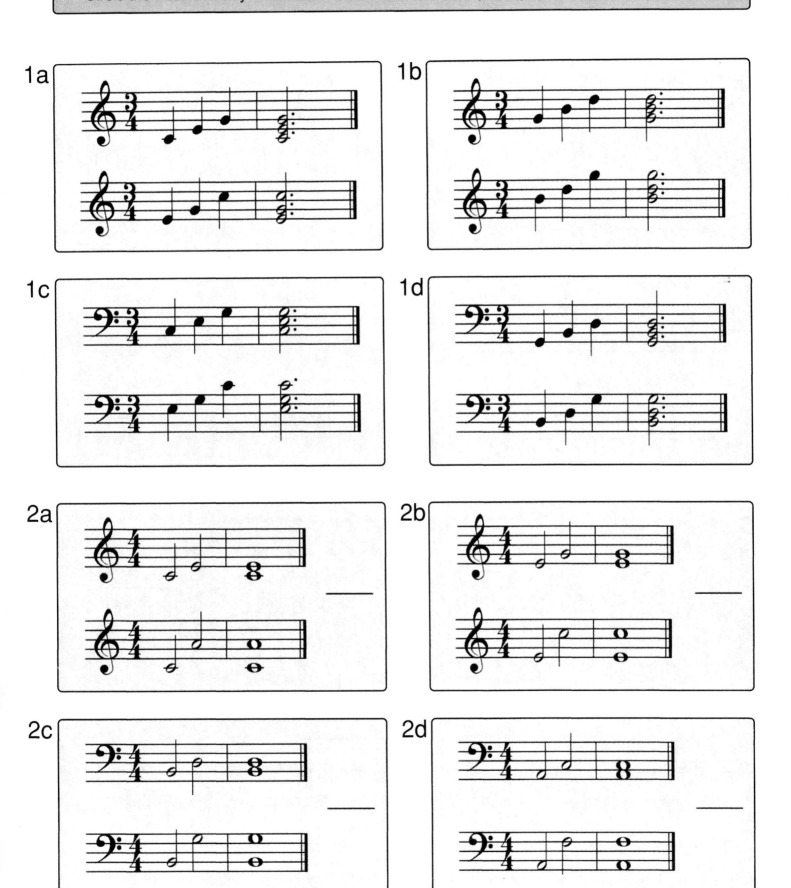

Use with pages 16–17.

TRIADS: The 2nd Inversion

1. Your teacher will play 1st INVERSION or 2nd INVERSION chords.
   Circle the example that you hear.
2. Your teacher will clap a rhythm pattern.
   Add a curved line for each tie that you hear.

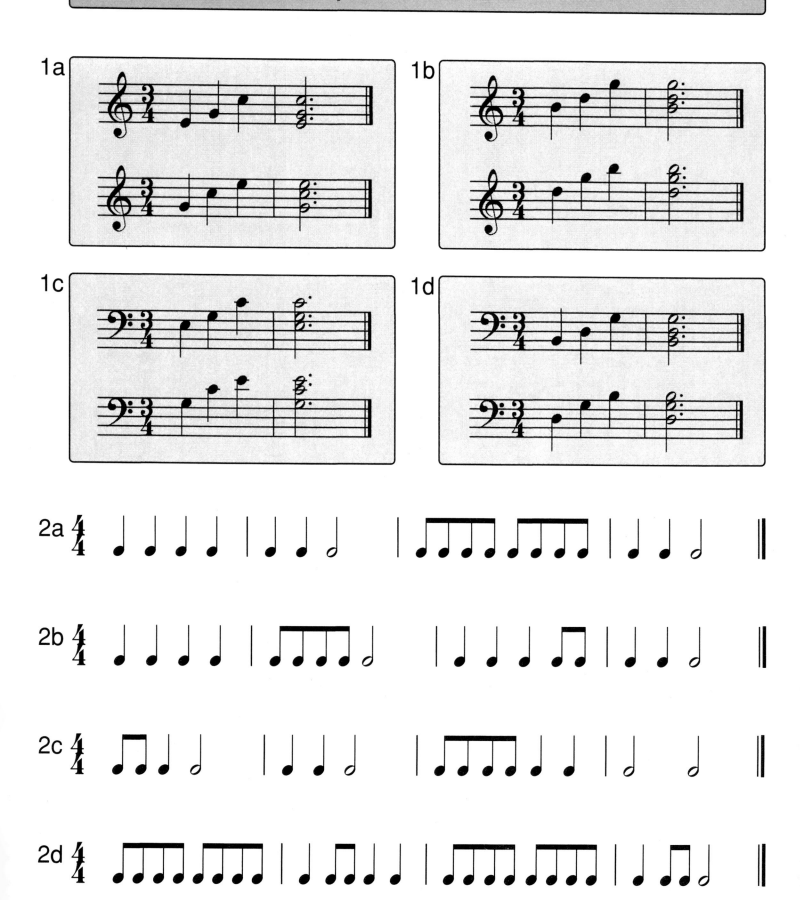

Major Scales

1. Your teacher will play MAJOR SCALES that move in PARALLEL or CONTRARY MOTION. Circle PARALLEL if the scales move in the SAME direction. Circle CONTRARY if the scales move in OPPOSITE directions.

2. Your teacher will play melodies that use notes from the C, G, D and F MAJOR SCALES. Draw the missing notes in the second measure, using the correct rhythm.

1a

PARALLEL

CONTRARY

1b

PARALLEL

CONTRARY

1c

PARALLEL

CONTRARY

1d

PARALLEL

CONTRARY

Use with page 19.

Syncopated Notes

1. Your teacher will clap a rhythm pattern.
   Draw the missing notes in the third measure, using

2. Your teacher will play a scale.
   • Add a CRESCENDO sign (<) UNDER the staff if the scale gets GRADUALLY LOUDER.
   • Add a DIMINUENDO sign (>) UNDER the staff if the scale gets GRADUALLY SOFTER.

TEACHER: See page 41.

Melody and Intervals

1. Your teacher will play four melodies. Two notes in each melody will be played incorrectly.
   Circle the incorrect notes.
2. Your teacher will play groups of HARMONIC intervals.
   Circle the group of intervals that you hear.

Use with page 22.

Seventh Chords

1. Your teacher will play a MAJOR triad or a SEVENTH chord.
   Circle MAJOR if you hear a MAJOR triad. Circle SEVENTH if you hear a SEVENTH chord.
2. Your teacher will play intervals of a 5th or 7th.
   Circle the interval that you hear. Write the interval name (5 or 7) on the line.

1a

M A J O R

S E V E N T H

1b

M A J O R

S E V E N T H

1c

M A J O R

S E V E N T H

1d

M A J O R

S E V E N T H

2a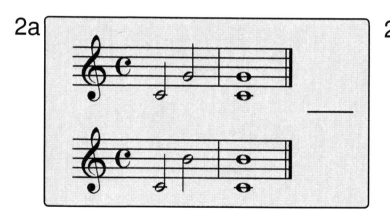

2b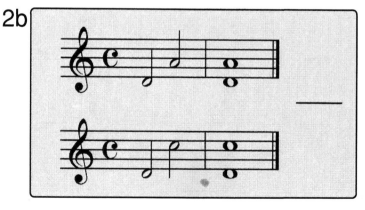

2c

2d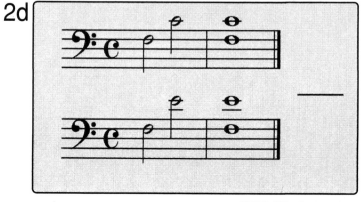

TEACHER: See page 42.

Seventh Chords

1. Your teacher will play groups of SEVENTH chords.
   Circle the group of chords that you hear.

2. Your teacher will play a BLOCK SEVENTH chord followed by a BROKEN SEVENTH chord.
   Write the notes of the BROKEN chord in the order that they are played, using QUARTER NOTES.

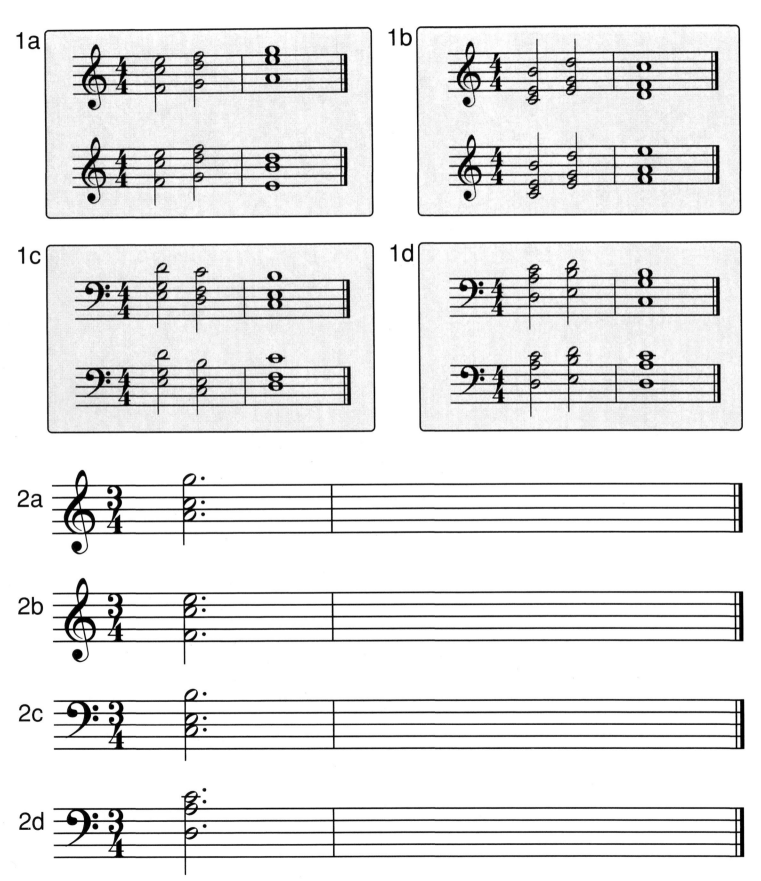

TEACHER: See page 42.

18

Inversions of Seventh Chords

Use with pages 24–25.

1. Your teacher will play a chord progression.
   Circle the progression that you hear.
2. Your teacher will clap a rhythm pattern.
   Draw the missing notes in the second measure, using ♩ ♩. ♩ ♫ or ♪

1a

1b

1c

1d

2a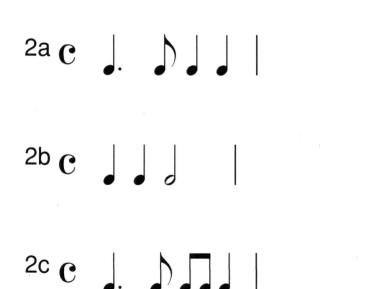

2b

2c

2d

TEACHER: See page 42.

Use with page 26.

The Key of E Minor

1. Your teacher will play the E NATURAL MINOR SCALE or the E HARMONIC MINOR SCALE.
   If the scale is HARMONIC MINOR, draw a SHARP (♯) in front of the 7th tones.

2. Your teacher will play the E NATURAL MINOR SCALE or the E MELODIC MINOR SCALE.
   If the scale is MELODIC MINOR, raise the 6th and 7th tones one half step (to C♯ and D♯) in the
   ASCENDING SCALE.

TEACHER: See page 42.

20

The Key of E Minor

1. Your teacher will play a BLOCK chord followed by a BROKEN chord.
   Write the notes of the BROKEN chord in the order that they are played, using QUARTER NOTES.
2. Your teacher will play intervals of a 6th, 7th or 8th (octave) ABOVE the given note from the
   E HARMONIC MINOR SCALE.
   • Draw the second note on the staff, using a half note.
   • Write the interval name (6, 7 or 8) on the line.

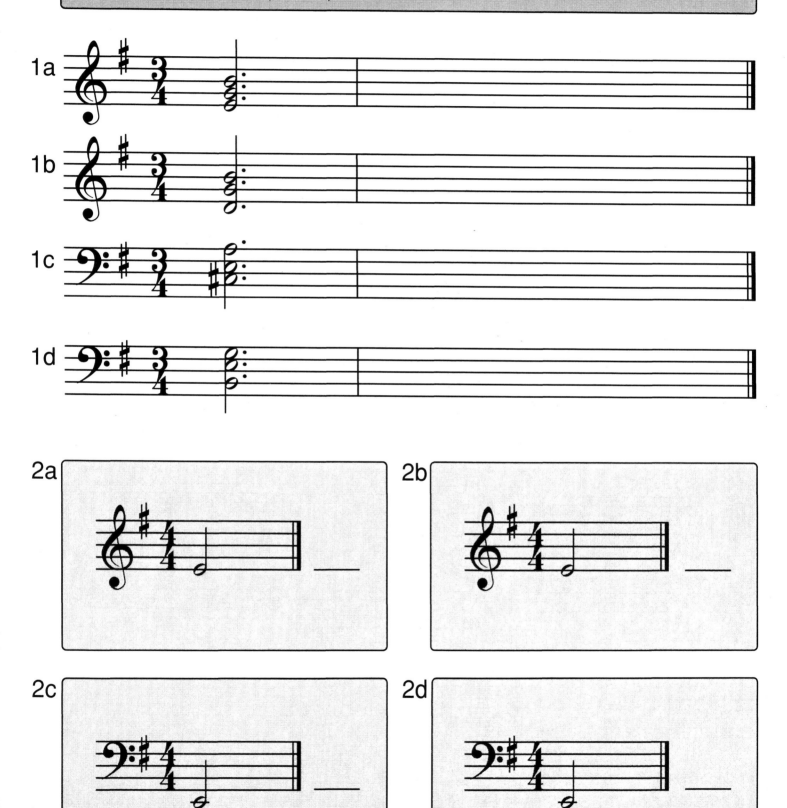

Primary Chords in E Minor

1. Your teacher will play **i**, **iv** and **V⁷** chords in the key of E minor.
   Write the Roman numeral name for each chord. The first chord is shown.

2. Your teacher will play a chord progression.
   Circle the progression that you hear.

1a   **i**   _____   _____   _____

1b   **iv**   _____   _____   _____

1c   **V7**   _____   _____   _____

1d   **iv**   _____   _____   _____

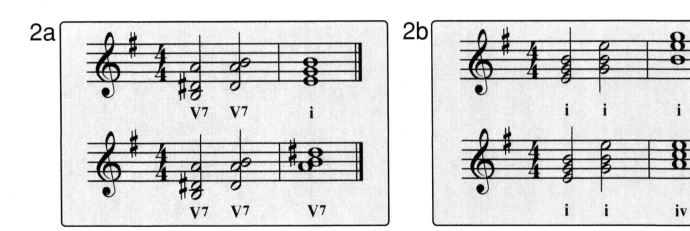

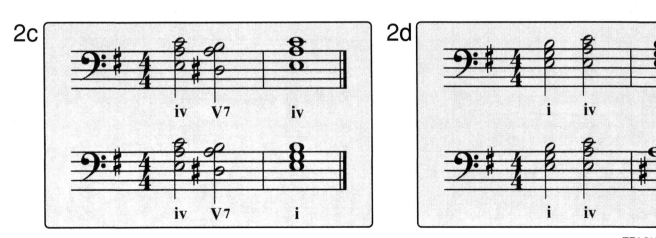

TEACHER: See page 43.

Use with page 30.

Sixteenth Notes

1. Your teacher will clap a rhythm pattern.
   Draw the missing notes in the second measure, using ♫♫♫♫ or ♩♩♫♫♫♫

2. Your teacher will play MELODIC intervals of a 6th, 7th or 8th (octave) ABOVE the given note.
   • Draw the second note on the staff, using a quarter note.
   • Write the interval name (6, 7 or 8) on the line.

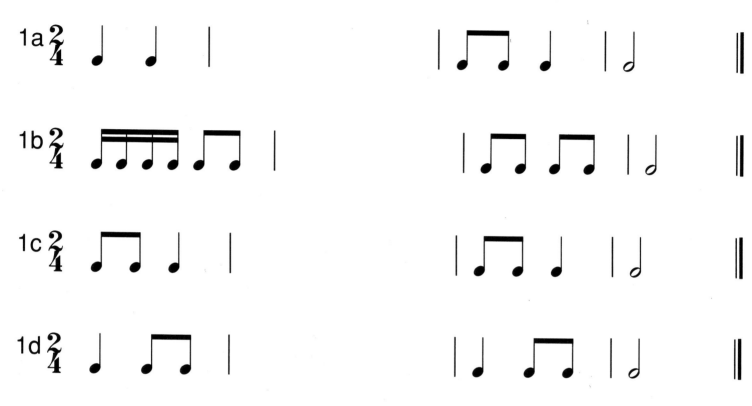

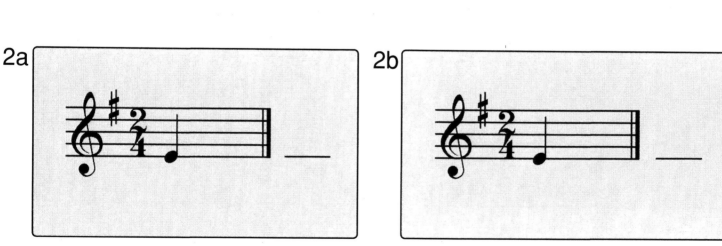

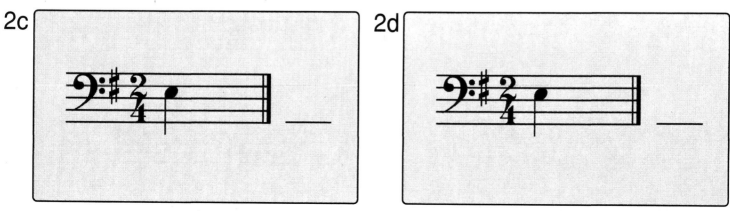

TEACHER: See page 43.

Sixteenth Notes

1. Your teacher will clap a rhythm pattern.
   Draw the missing notes in the second measure, using ♩ ♫♫ ♫ or ♬ ♬
2. Your teacher will play a left hand accompaniment pattern.
   Circle the pattern that you hear.

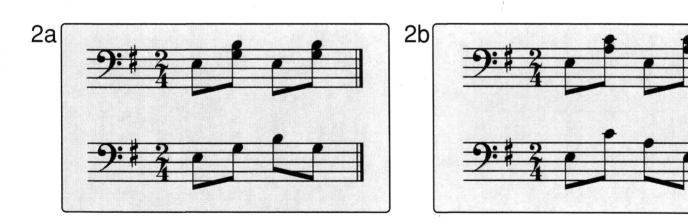

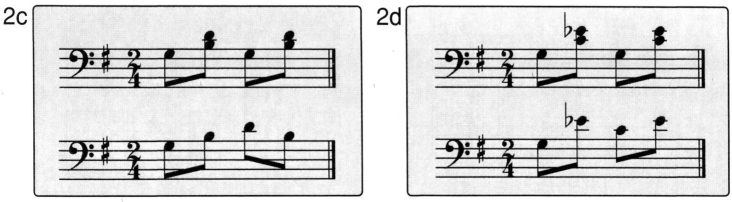

Use with pages 32–33.

Sixteenth Notes

1. Your teacher will clap a rhythm pattern.
   Circle the pattern that you hear.
2. Your teacher will play a chord progression.
   Circle the progression that you hear.

1a

1b

1c

1d

2a

2b
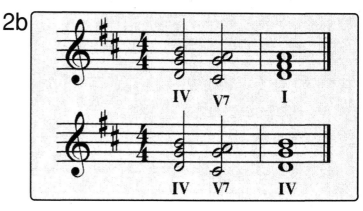

2c
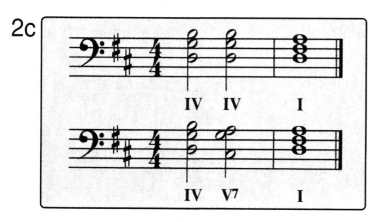

2d
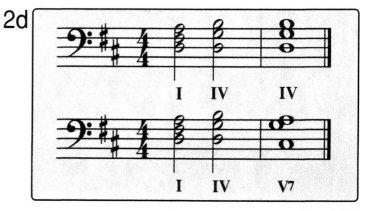

TEACHER: See page 44.

The Dotted Eighth Note

1. Your teacher will clap a rhythm pattern.
   Draw the missing notes in the box, using ♪♪ or ♪.♪
2. Your teacher will clap a rhythm pattern.
   Circle the pattern that you hear.

1a

1b

1c

1d

2a

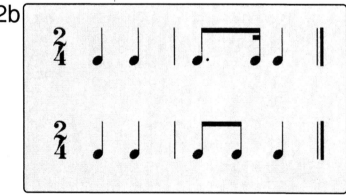

2b

2c

2d

TEACHER: See page 44.

Use with page 36.

The B♭ Major Scale

1. Your teacher will play B♭ MAJOR SCALES. One note in each scale will be played incorrectly. Circle the incorrect note.

2. Your teacher will play B♭ MAJOR SCALES that move in PARALLEL or CONTRARY motion. Circle PARALLEL if the scales move in the SAME direction. Circle CONTRARY if the scales move in OPPOSITE directions.

2a
PARALLEL

CONTRARY

2b
PARALLEL

CONTRARY

2c
PARALLEL

CONTRARY

2d
PARALLEL

CONTRARY

TEACHER: See page 44.

The B♭ Major Scale

1. Your teacher will play melodies that use notes from the B♭ MAJOR SCALE.
   Draw the missing notes in the second measure, using the correct rhythm.

2. Your teacher will play B♭ MAJOR SCALES.
   Circle the rhythm pattern that you hear for each scale.

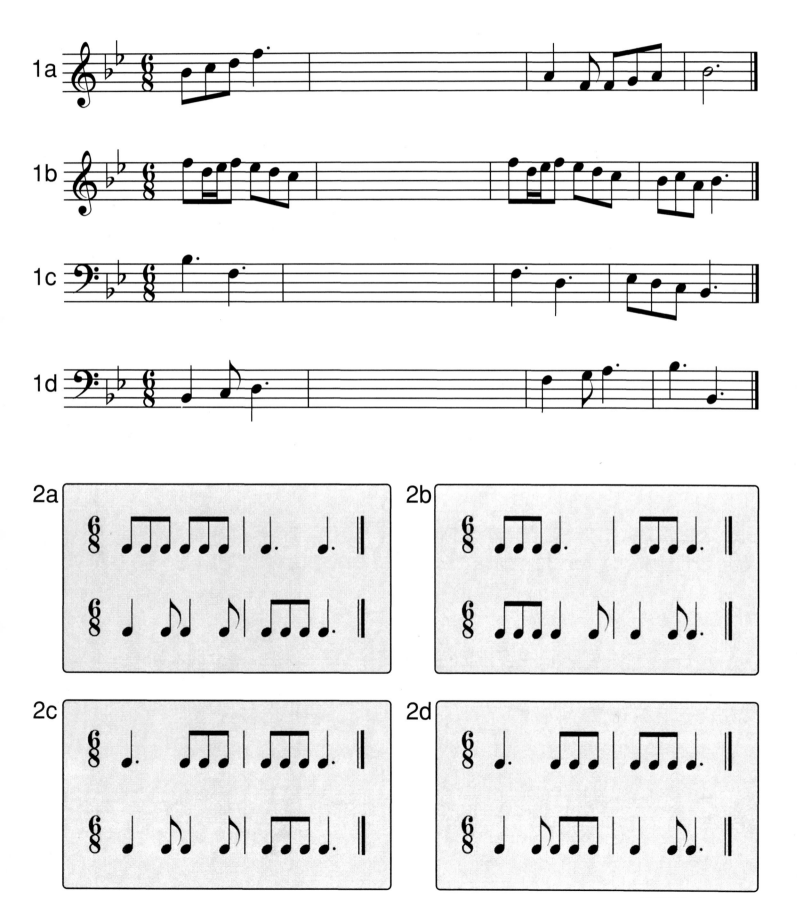

Use with pages 38–39.

Primary Chords in B♭ Major

1. Your teacher will play a BLOCK chord followed by a BROKEN chord.
   Write the notes of the BROKEN chord in the order that they are played, using QUARTER notes.

2. Your teacher will play melodies and chords in B♭ major.
   Write the Roman numeral names (**I**, **IV** or **V⁷**) on the lines below the staff.

The Key of G Minor

1. Your teacher will play the G NATURAL MINOR SCALE or the G HARMONIC MINOR SCALE.
   If the scale is HARMONIC MINOR, draw a SHARP (♯) in front of the 7th tones.

2. Your teacher will play the G NATURAL MINOR SCALE or the G MELODIC MINOR SCALE.
   If the scale is MELODIC MINOR, raise the 6th and 7th tones one half step (to E♮ and F♯) in the
   ASCENDING SCALE.

Use with page 41.

The Key of G Minor

1. Your teacher will play melodies from the G HARMONIC MINOR SCALE.
   Draw the missing notes in the second measure, using the correct rhythm.

2. Your teacher will clap a rhythm pattern.
   Draw the missing notes in the second measure, using ♩ ♪♪ ♩ or ♩. ♪

Primary Chords in G Minor

1. Your teacher will play **i**, **iv** and **V⁷** chords in the key of G minor.
   Write the Roman numeral name for each chord. The first chord is shown.
2. Your teacher will play a chord progression.
   Circle the progression that you hear.

1a   **iv**   _____   _____   _____

1b   **i**   _____   _____   _____

1c   **V⁷**   _____   _____   _____

1d   **iv**   _____   _____   _____

2a
i   iv   V⁷

i   iv   iv

2b

V⁷   V⁷   V⁷

V⁷   V⁷   V⁷

2c
iv   i   V⁷

iv   V⁷   i

2d

V⁷   V⁷   V⁷

V⁷   V⁷   V⁷

Use with page 43.

Primary Chords in G Minor

1. Your teacher will play a left hand accompaniment pattern.
   Circle the pattern that you hear.

2. Your teacher will play melodies and broken chords in G minor.
   Write the Roman numeral names (**i**, **iv** or **V⁷**) on the lines below the staff.

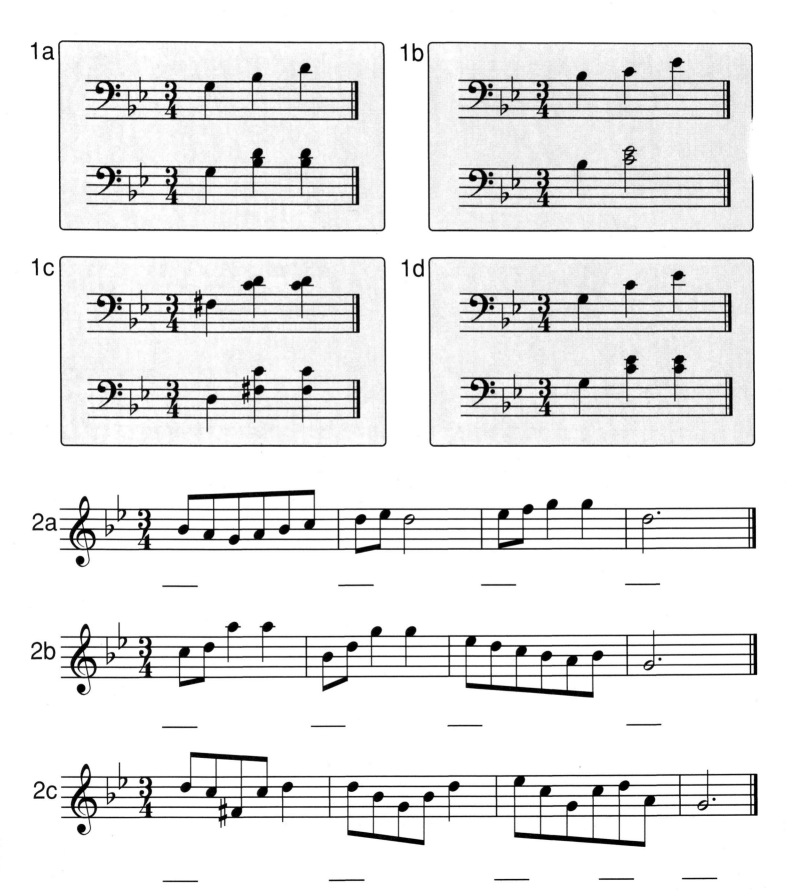

Harmonic Minor Scales

1. Your teacher will play A, E, D and G HARMONIC MINOR SCALES. One note in each scale will be played incorrectly. Circle the incorrect note.

2. Your teacher will play melodies that use notes from the A, E, D and G HARMONIC MINOR SCALES. Draw the missing notes in the second measure, using the correct rhythm.

34

Use with page 45.

Intervals

1. Your teacher will play intervals of a 6th, 7th or 8th (octave) ABOVE the given note from the
G HARMONIC MINOR SCALE.
   • Draw the second note on the staff, using a half note.
   • Write the interval name (6, 7 or 8) on the line.

2. Your teacher will play groups of HARMONIC intervals.
   Circle the group of intervals that you hear.

1a

1b

1c

1d

2a

2b

2c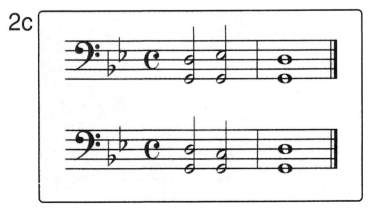

2d

TEACHER: See page 48.

Sixteenth Notes

1. Your teacher will clap a rhythm pattern.
   Draw the missing notes in the second measure, using
2. Your teacher will play four accompaniment patterns. Each pattern contains two ACCENTS.
   Add an ACCENT SIGN (>) over the notes that are played LOUDER.

36

Review

1. Your teacher will clap a rhythm pattern.
   Circle the pattern that you hear.

2. Your teacher will play **i**, **iv** and **V**^{7} chords in the key of E minor.
   Write the Roman numeral name for each chord. The first chord is shown.

3. Your teacher will play the G NATURAL MINOR SCALE or the G HARMONIC MINOR SCALE.
   If the scale is HARMONIC MINOR, draw a SHARP (♯) in front of the 7th tone.

4. Your teacher will play a chord progression.
   Circle the progression that you hear.

5. Your teacher will play a group of HARMONIC intervals.
   Circle the group of intervals that you hear.

1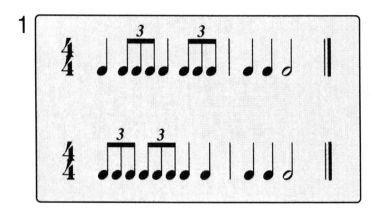

2 **iv** _____ _____ _____

3

4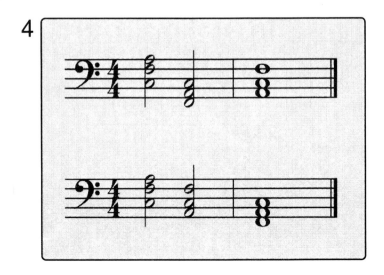

5

Review

1. Your teacher will clap a rhythm pattern.
   Draw the missing notes in the second measure, using [♩] [♪♪] [♫] or [♬]

2. Your teacher will play a BLOCK chord followed by a BROKEN chord.
   Write the notes of the BROKEN chord in the order that they are played, using QUARTER NOTES.

3. Your teacher will play a melody that uses notes from the B♭ MAJOR SCALE.
   Draw the missing notes in the second measure, using the correct rhythm.

4. Your teacher will play a BLOCK SEVENTH chord followed by a BROKEN SEVENTH chord.
   Write the notes of the BROKEN chord in the order that they are played, using QUARTER NOTES.

5. Your teacher will play an interval of a 6th, 7th or 8th (octave) ABOVE the given note from the
   E HARMONIC MINOR SCALE.
   • Draw the second note on the staff, using a half note.
   • Write the interval name (6, 7 or 8) on the line.

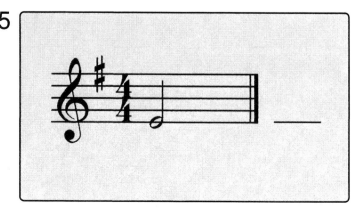

38

Teacher's Examples

Page 3 (Clap)

Page 4 (Clap)   (Play)

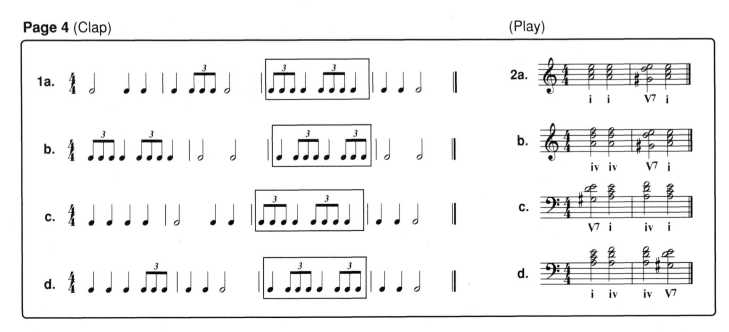

Teacher's Examples

Page 5 (Play)

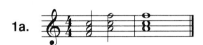

Page 6 (Play)

Page 7 (Play)

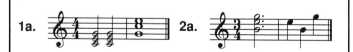
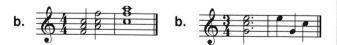

Page 8 (Play)

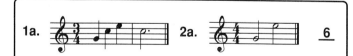
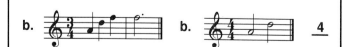

40

Teacher's Examples

Page 9 (Play)

Page 10 (Play)   **Page 11** (Play)

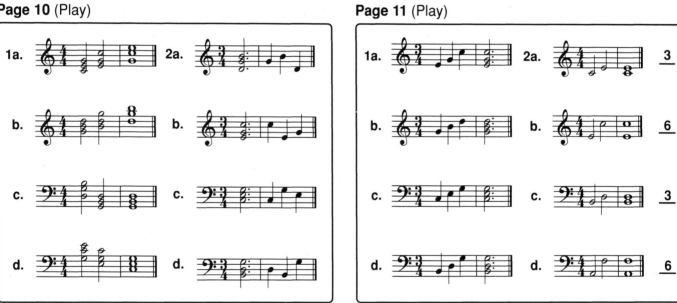

Page 12 (Play)   (Clap)

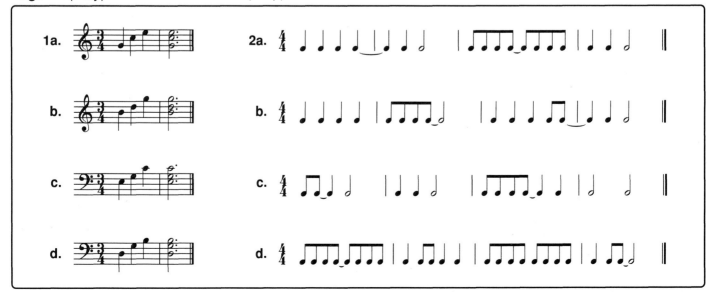

Teacher's Examples

Page 13 (Play)

Page 14 (Clap)   (Play)

Page 15 (Play)

42

Teacher's Examples

Page 16 (Play)

Page 17 (Play)

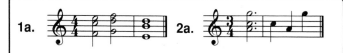

Page 18 (Play)   (Clap)

Page 19 (Play)

Teacher's Examples

Page 20 (Play) **Page 21** (Play)

Page 22 (Clap)   (Play)

Page 23 (Clap)   (Play)

44

Teacher's Examples

Page 24 (Clap)

(Play)

Page 25 (Clap)

Page 26 (Play)

Teacher's Examples

Page 27 (Play)

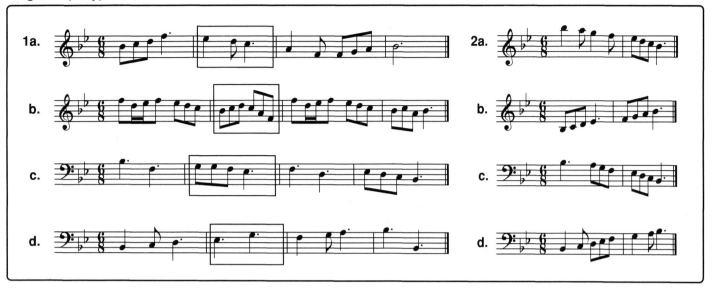

Page 28 (Play)

Teacher's Examples

Page 29 (Play)

Page 30 (Play)   (Clap)

Teacher's Examples

Page 31 (Play)

Page 32 (Play)

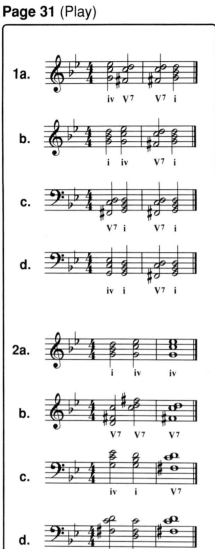

Page 33 (Play)

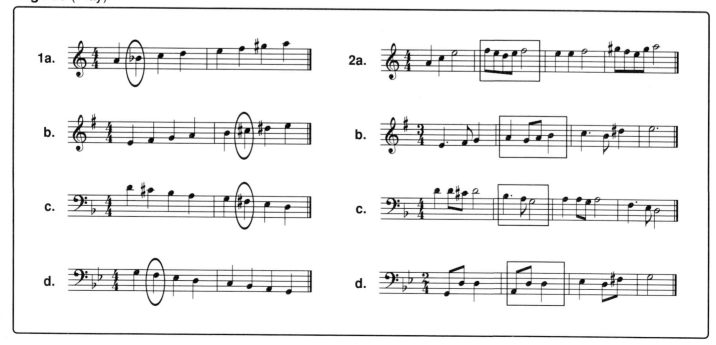

48

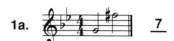

Teacher's Examples

Page 34 (Play)

1a. ... 7

b. ... 6

c. ... 7

d. ... 8

2a.

b.

c.

d.

Page 35 (Clap)

1a.

b.

c.

d.

(Play)

2a.

b.

c.

d.

Page 36 (Clap)

1.

(Play)

2. iv V⁷ V⁷ i

3.

4.

5.

Page 37 (Clap)

1.

(Play)

2.

3.

4.

5. ... 7